Sherman The Therapy Dog

Jim Burris

DEDICATION

This book is dedicated to Sherry.

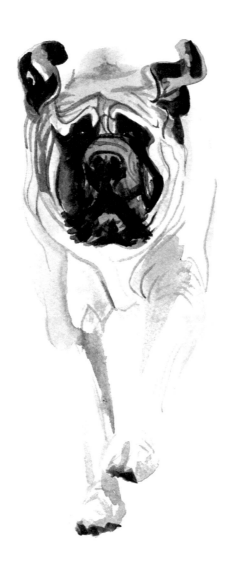

When Sherry McAllister decided to add another therapy dog to her family, an English Mastiff was the obvious choice. The McAllisters had a lot of experience and success with the breed and were eager to move forward in this new phase of their life.

Sherry did a lot of research trying to find the best possible breeder. While she typically adopts dogs, Sherry wanted to ensure a healthy bloodline and solid reputation of producing breed standard puppies.

The chosen breeder from Reno, Nevada is well known for top quality standards and practices.

The best therapy dogs exhibit specific traits and characteristics before training begins. Disposition, attitude and play style are closely examined and evaluated to confirm they are the best candidates.

Sherry received a call from her breeder announcing the choice for her therapy dog! One of the puppies stood out from the bunch! He greeted the human in the room instead of running to the food bowl. He interacted gently and safely with children.

Sherman The Therapy Dog arrived. The adoption took place when Sherman was twenty two pounds and eight weeks old.

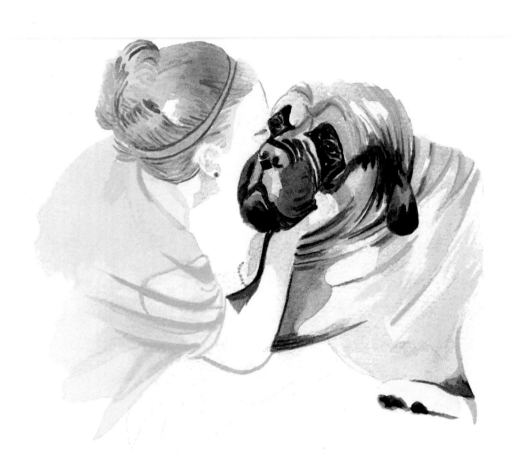

There are a lot of differences between service dogs and therapy dogs therefore the training differs greatly. While both require certain disposition standards and behavior patterns. A service dog is trained to assist and protect one person. The dog will live with that person and become an integral part of their life. A therapy dog is trained to serve a wide range of people in many settings.

Sherman began his training and earned his good citizen certification at sixteen weeks of age. Sherry owns Big Love Therapy group which specializes in training therapy dogs. The focus is on the human/animal bond and training them as a team . The goal is to harness the strength of the duo and attain full knowledge of their positive benefits. Boundaries and limitations are established. The objective is to encourage and motivate the desired behavior and understand the dog's emotions, body language and communication skills.

Major exposure to wheelchairs and medical devices, how to approach a bed, where to stand and how to greet are part of the program. Sherman was trained to serve in several type of therapy settings which include hospice, special needs and long term care facilities. He is quite effective in nursing homes, private homes and extended care facilities. He works with day care programs for children and adults. In a hospice situation Sherman is called upon to bring peace and comfort to a family experiencing the final days of a loved one. Stress and anxiety can be a major problem during those difficult times. Sherman's size and manners always attract the attention of everyone in the room!

Sherman's presence can change and redirect a chaotic situation into peace and harmony.

In one situation where there was tension and disagreement Sherman was able to bring joy and laughter. The family discussion shifted from finances and trouble to running on the beach with their dogs long ago.

Memory care unit residents can be filled with confusion, panic, anger and sadness. A therapy dog can shatter that dark cloud, even if it's just for a brief moment. Often times there is non-verbal communication between the resident and Sherman. A simple touch can change everything and usually does.

In the children and adult day programs Sherman can bring a calming effect. Which is much needed to maintain their attention. Sherman and Sherry are internationally known and loved for their selfless acts of love and kindness. They are regularly called upon to make special appearances at pet supply stores and fundraisers for animals in need. They attend school functions and activities.

During Sherman's third year of therapy work, tragic news came to the McAllister family. Sherry was diagnosed with an aggressive form of cancer. Everything was about to change.

The story spread quickly through social media and the therapy community. Sherry underwent major surgery, followed by long term aftercare treatment, which resulted in side effect sickness, long periods of sleep and full bed rest. Sherman knew what to do! He inched his way to Sherry's bed, the person who taught him everything he knows about caring for a person in need.

Sherman didn't leave Sherry's bedside for one year while she struggled. He lay his head on her hand to let her know he was there. Sherry would feel safe and protected while listening to the familiar sound of his breathing and snoring. Sherry didn't waste a moment while recuperating in that bed. She forced herself to work serving others, of course. She worked on the annual Sherman calendar and kept their worldwide friends updated. Healing began.

While transitioning from the immobilizing state back to the therapy work Sherry could barely walk. Many times she required a wheelchair and Sherman walked proudly alongside. Sherman was giving his owner the same support and encouragement he had always received from her. She needed to regain strength and return to what she loves most…being a beautiful message of hope, love and happiness. Sherry and Sherman's work continues, although it is not always easy. She navigates the very difficult journey and she is winning!

Sherry was once told of an elderly resident in a care facility who didn't speak and rarely left their room. Sherry and Sherman responded to the call, heading to the room to help. One year later that same resident wants to be notified each time Sherman is scheduled to visit…and they wait in the hallway with a smile. Whether it's the feel of the fur on his back or his cold, wet nose or simply the sounds of Sherman sleeping…he transcends earthly problems to bring peace, happiness, a moment of freedom and sometimes a tear of joy.

A NOTE FROM THE AUTHOR

I created these illustrations using watercolor. Beautiful reproductions are available. For information on how to purchase the 12x18 prints please send me an email at

tattoojims@gmail.com

Thank you for your interest. Wishing you peace and happiness!

61489779R00020

Made in the USA
San Bernardino, CA
14 December 2017